I0763025

Caleb Fellowes

FOUNDER OF THE

Fellowes Athenaeum

DIED NOV. 8TH 1852.

DEDICATION SERVICES

OF

THE FELLOWES ATHENÆUM

AND THE

Roxbury Branch of the Boston Public Library,

JULY 9th, 1873.

PREPARED BY THE SUPERINTENDENT OF THE PUBLIC LIBRARY.

BOSTON:
PRINTED FOR THE FELLOWES ATHENÆUM.
ROCKWELL & CHURCHILL, CITY PRINTERS.
1873.

TRUSTEES AND OFFICERS, 1873.

Trustees of the Fellowes Athenæum.

GEORGE PUTNAM, D. D., PRESIDENT.

GEORGE PUTNAM, ...	130 Highland Street, ...	*President.*
SUPPLY C. THWING, ...	175 Highland Street, ...	*Treasurer.*
JOHN F. OSGOOD, ...	Guild Street, ...	*Secretary.*
WILLIAM WHITING, ...	Walnut Park.	
JOSEPH S. ROPES, ...	60 State Street.	
NATHANIEL J. BRADLEE, . . .	65 Highland Street.	
SAMUEL C. COBB, ...	120 Highland Street.	
CHARLES K. DILLAWAY, ...	2095 Washington Street.	
WILLIAM C. COLLAR, ...	25 Thornton Street.	
EDWARD E. HALE, ...	39 Highland Street.	

Trustees of the Public Library.

WILLIAM W. GREENOUGH, PRESIDENT.

JOHN T. CLARK, ...	43 Commonwealth Avenue, .	*Alderman.*
WILLIAM E. PERKINS, ...	83 Mount Vernon Street, . .	*Councilman.*
CHARLES A. BURDITT, ...	Mill Street, Ward 16, . .	"
GEORGE PUTNAM, ...	130 Highland Street, ...	*At Large.*
WESTON LEWIS, ...	81 Worcester Street, ...	"
WILLIAM W. GREENOUGH, . .	56 Temple Street, ...	"
GEORGE S. HILLARD, ...	62 Pinckney Street, ...	"
SAMUEL A. GREEN, ...	25 Kneeland Street, ...	"
DANIEL S. CURTIS, ...	214 Beacon Street, ...	"

General Officers of the Public Library.

JUSTIN WINSOR, SUPERINTENDENT AND SECRETARY OF THE TRUSTEES.
WILLIAM A. WHEELER, *Assistant Superintendent.*
JAMES L. WHITNEY, *Principal Assistant.*

Roxbury Branch.

Miss H. C. PRICE, *Librarian.*
Mrs. JULIA A. NYE, *Reading Room Assistant.*
Miss MARIETTA GOLDSMITH, *Delivery Assistant.*
MARGARET A. BLOOD, *Runner.*
CHARLES R. CURTIS, *Janitor.*

SERVICES.

THE committees charged with making preparations for the services in commemoration of the union of the FELLOWES ATHENÆUM and the ROXBURY BRANCH of the PUBLIC LIBRARY of the city of Boston, and for the dedication of the new library building on Millmont street, consisted, on the part of the Athenæum, of SAMUEL C. COBB, NATHANIEL J. BRADLEE and SUPPLY C. THWING, Esquires; and on the part of the Public Library, of the special committee on the Roxbury Branch, of which WILLIAM W. GREENOUGH, Esq., the President of the Trustees, was chairman, and the REV. GEORGE PUTNAM, D. D., the HON. GEORGE S. HILLARD, WESTON LEWIS, Esq., and CHARLES A. BURDITT, Esq., were the other members.

Invitations were extended in the name of the two boards to prominent citizens of Roxbury, and of the city Government, and to a few others, and public announcement having been made, the assembling of the guests and others took place in the Reading Room of the Library building, in the second story, which was arranged for the occasion. A portrait in oil of CALEB FELLOWES, the founder of the Athenæum, having been deposited by S. C. THWING, Esq., with the Athenæum, it was hung on the wall of the room, in view of the audience.

The hour appointed for the beginning of the ceremonies was half-past three, when his Honor, HENRY L. PIERCE, MAYOR OF BOSTON, entered the hall, and took his seat on the platform, as presiding officer of the occasion. He was accompanied by the gentlemen who were to share with him in the exercises.

The MAYOR called upon the Reverend A. C. THOMPSON, D. D., of the Eliot Church, to offer prayer.

The MAYOR then spoke as follows: —

MR. PRESIDENT, LADIES AND GENTLEMEN: — The consummation of the union of private beneficence with public liberality, such as we have now met to celebrate, and the establishment of this library, must exercise a great and beneficent influence upon the people who reside in this locality, now and in the future. There can be no more noble or useful institution than a Public Library, which is open to all, and to which all have the freest access. I congratulate the citizens of Roxbury upon the auspicious conclusion of the labors of their own citizens and the co-operation of the City Government in the establishment of this institution.

JOHN FELT OSGOOD, Esq., the Secretary of the Board of Trustees of the Fellowes Athenæum and Chairman of the Committee which had had charge of the construction of the edifice, then delivered the keys of the building (the President of the Trustees of the Public Library standing to receive them), in the following words: —

On behalf of the Trustees it becomes my duty to deliver to you, sir, the keys and custody of this building. And in thus cementing the union of the Fellowes Athenæum with the Public Library, we would indulge the hope that such union shall prove so strong and lasting that future generations will remember with gratitude the generosity of Caleb and Sarah Fellowes, through whom we are possessed of these lands, buildings and volumes; and as well remember the care of that Municipal Government which seeks, by the establishment of its Branch Library here, to secure to this district a brighter future, by giving to all classes a full opportunity to enlighten and cultivate the mind.

WILLIAM W. GREENOUGH, Esq., President of the Trustees of the Public Library, responded as follows: —

MR. MAYOR, LADIES AND GENTLEMEN: — In the preface to De Morgan's Book upon Paradoxes I find these words: "But there may be, and are, those who want books, and cannot pay the (Royal) Society's price. The council would be very liberal in allowing their books to be consulted. I have no doubt that if a known investigator were to call and to ask to look at certain books, the Assistant Secretary would forthwith seat him with the books before him, absence of F. R. S. (Fellow of the Royal Society) not in any wise withstanding. But this is not like having the right to consult any book, on any day, and to take it away, if further wanted."

This short paragraph opens, to the American reader, the differences which exist, in the uses of books, in the old collections of Europe and the free libraries of England and of the New World. It shows the lines which have limited, and fenced round, the applications for knowledge in those who were not to the "manner born," or who had not achieved the distinction, by their merits, of obtaining ready access to the stores of learning needed for the extension of their accomplishments. No one in these days will agree that such precautions are necessary to protect the innumerable books which the industry or the vanity of man have caused to be printed, and of which one may conjecture, without any uncharitable motive, that few have issued from the press without an opinion on the part of the author, that, some time or other, whether in the present or in the future, the contents of the volume would be of value to some one or more persons, in their day or generation. To the general reader of the present day, living four centuries, or more, since the discovery of the art of printing, it is not remarkable that so many geniuses have mistaken their vocation, and have not appreciated the doctrine of the wisest of the ancients, that "of making many books there is no end."

But it is for a directly personal relation that libraries are founded here. One could not but be impressed by, and deplore deeply, the losses to human knowledge that came of the destruction of the libraries of France during the Prussian and the civil war. Manuscripts of which no copies exist, the rarest of books, specimens of many of the most costly bindings and most beautiful *chefs-d'œuvre* of the art of printing, perished in the flames. Other private libraries were stolen by the invading forces, with the same scent of plunder which too often distinguishes the march of armies. In any event, the books and manuscripts burned or stolen could not be replaced.

In contrasting this condition of affairs with our own, it must be a subject of measurable rejoicing, that, while few of our libraries have the opportunity to gather such priceless treasures, they contain, for the most part, modern and standard books, in which are summed up the results of the aggregated wisdom and learning of the ages, and which, even if destroyed by fire, may be replaced without permanent hindrance to the progression of the communities whose daily wants they supply. One may regret deeply the effacing of such relics of the past as are part of the history of the race, as illustrate its civilization, or its social progress, as form part of the knowledge, which research and scholarship add to human accomplishments; but equally if not more important are the text-books and the treatises which sum up for modern necessities the experiences of bygone centuries, to which have been added the inventions, discoveries and adaptations to present existences of the men who write and print in these days of steam and electric velocity.

In receiving from you, MR. CHAIRMAN, the keys of this new temple, to be hereafter devoted to the purposes I have just designated, — a repository of standard knowledge and advancement, — on behalf of the Trustees of the Public Library, I pay grateful reverence to the memory of Caleb and Sarah Fellowes, and most heartily return thanks to the Trustees of the Fellowes Athenæum, as well as to the City of Boston, who have jointly given to us the power to establish, in the old town of Roxbury, now part of our own metropolis, a Library worthy of so active and intelligent a population. We accept the trust with a full cognizance of the responsibility which it entails, feeling secure that, if the principles upon which our own great Library in the city was founded, and upon which it has prospered to an extraordinary degree, are true and lasting, their application to this new centre of power and cultivation will be also successful.

What, then, is the character of the institution now to be dedicated to the uses of your residents? Owing to the wisdom of the Fellowes bequest, there is now established a Branch nearer in grade to the great Central Library than has before been practicable. There is, however, this difference, that here all books, except works of reference required for purposes of consultation within the building, will be free for circulation, thus bringing with the gradual growth of its higher department, within immediate reach, the large class of works of permanent and substantial value which at present belong, and in the future will be added, to the Bates Hall Collection.

By the liberal compact between the Fellowes Trustees and the City of Boston, this Branch will be governed by the same regulations that are in force in East and South Boston, and which are identical with those which have been found proper and necessary in the administration of the Central Library. The same freedom of access will exist. But, above and beyond this, the residents of the Highland district will enjoy a larger privilege than is allotted to the other precincts. While both portions of this library are open to their use, at the same time they also have permission to borrow from the Bates Hall such books as circulate, and are not to be found in the smaller collection at home.

One of the results of the formation of libraries upon the Boston system has been the invaluable indication given by each community of the description of books which it needs and will read. Classes of books which remain untouched upon the shelves in one locality are of large service in another. Periodicals of popular interest in one Branch Reading Room find few or no readers in another. In the founding of a general Library, it is both natural and convenient that it should include within its purchasing power the largest number of books useful to the largest number of people. These are sufficiently indicated by the experience gained from the establishment of the great variety of free libraries already in successful progress. But beyond this, each neighborhood is expected to ask for such works, not already provided, as are within the pecuniary means of the institution. By this method the sympathy and aid of all classes of readers will in time be secured.

In the plan of this elegant structure, now devoted to popular service, separate arrangements have been made for the youth and adults, a want largely felt in the Central Library, where the attendance of juvenile readers often interferes with the comfort of their seniors. But, beyond this, one may congratulate the Fellowes Trustees upon the erection of a building, for the uses of the public, combining the best results of modern skill, and, for its size and capacity, one may justly say, fully equal if not superior, in its conveniences, to any structure for the purpose hitherto built. The general plan of the interior is due to the Superintendent of the Public Library as modified by the large experience of the accomplished architect.

I have but a word more to say. This new Library starts into existence with larger and more permanent foundations than were vouchsafed to the parent Library. Its small beginnings were fashioned into consistent form by the generosity of Mr. Bates, whose bounty still continues from his funded donation. At the outset, and for the future, this institution is to receive its most important additions from the ministration of the Fellowes bequest. When the steady increase of twenty years has brought to its present position the Central Library, may not one reasonably expect that a proportional growth and usefulness shall attend this fortunate beginning, and that the trust equally shared by the residents of Roxbury and the managers of the Branch, shall find full and grateful acceptance?

The MAYOR next introduced WILLIAM C. COLLAR, Esq., one of the Trustees of the Fellowes Athenæum, and Head Master of the Roxbury Latin School, who delivered the following address, making allusion as he began to the absence of the Reverend DOCTOR GEORGE PUTNAM, President of the Fellowes Trustees: —

MR. PRESIDENT, FRIENDS, AND FELLOW-CITIZENS OF ROXBURY: — The duty which has been assigned to me on this occasion by my associates upon the Board of Trustees is not an unpleasing one in itself, but to me it would have been embarrassing in any case, and it becomes peculiarly so from the circumstance that I am to speak in place of one to whom I have myself listened with rapture many times; in place of him to whose wise counsels this community has looked for instruction and guidance, and in whose eloquence it has taken pride and delight for more than forty years. But though I shrank from this task, I felt that his health was too precious to the public to which he has given the labor of his life, but which is by no means ready or willing to release him from its service — too precious, I say, to be imperilled in the least degree by the performance of any duty however slight. So you will not hear his voice to-day, and I greatly regret that we have not the encouragement, which his presence would give, to hope that his complete restoration will be but the work of a little longer time.

We have assembled to devote this building, with some simple ceremony, to interests only less exalted than those of religion itself; and we follow, in doing so, the custom of three thousand years, and the practice of nations whom we acknoweldge as our moral and intellectual guides and instructors. Perhaps I should say that we seem to be following an immemorial custom, but are in truth acting in obedience to a sentiment coeval with humanity, and not less universal; that sentiment which from the first taught men to see something divine in natural objects, rather to view as wholly divine, as gods, whatever created thing — sun, or sea, or cloud — seemed powerful to help and bountiful to bless; that sentiment which, instructed by reason, still loves to ascribe a sacredness, still loves to hallow by some public and formal act, works of man's labor and skill that are designed for immaterial and noble ends.

As you entered this building, you read the name "Athenæum" inscribed upon its front. The word, as you knew, means "temple of Athena," the Greek goddess of wisdom; and it may be that some of you thought of it as a strange anomaly that Christian people should assemble to consecrate with Christian prayer what by its name professed to be a temple to a heathen deity. And if this thought led you for a moment to dwell upon the past, you would naturally reflect upon the contrast which these halls will every day present, when compared with some sanctuary of Athena in old Athens twenty centuries ago and more — some temple as much inferior to this unpretending structure in deep significance and beneficent purpose, as surpassing it in costliness and outward splendor, — contrast which I can now only suggest, but which impressively marks and in some sense measures the difference between the life of that remote past and the life of to-day. As the patroness of letters, Athena's votaries did not include the lowly and the unlearned, women and youth, but philosophers and historians, poets and orators; these only resorted to her temples to seek her favor, or to read the productions which she had inspired. The gates of knowledge which we fling wide were barred to all but a favored few of one sex, and the priceless heritage of every child among us could be won only by birth, or genius or wealth. Truly on our lips "Athenæum" has a meaning far different from that of old; a meaning far higher and nobler. We choose it as the most fitting term to symbolize that wisdom and culture which it is the design and the promise of this institution to foster. With such an object, subserving such a purpose, who would exchange this plain and simple edifice of brick and stone for any glory of Pentelic marble, though wrought with the utmost skill of antiquity? And who would give the treasures of wisdom that will be gathered here, for the finest statue of ivory and gold ever conceived by the genius or carved by the hand of Phidias? "Athenæum," then, though applied so differently by us, is yet in this case no misnomer; and it is no slight recommendation of the name that it recalls to our minds a faith that once ruled the fairest parts of the earth, and inspired thoughts that will never perish. It suggests, too, a thousand graceful fancies, pleasing legends of her who was chief among many deities with which the imagination of the Greeks peopled the earth, the air and the waters; legends that still have a power to instruct as well as to please, though we smile at the superstitions they embody.

> "The intelligible forms of ancient poets,
> The fair humanities of old religion,
> The Power, the Beauty, and the Majesty,
> That had their haunts in dale, or piny mountain,
> Or forest, by slow stream, or pebbly spring,
> Or chasms and watery depths, — all these have vanished;
> They live no longer in the faith of reason."

But it is enough to have cast one momentary glance at that past which it is not well that we should ever forget, and of which the name that this institution bears will always so happily remind us. At this time your thoughts will more naturally turn to him whose portrait hangs upon this wall, whose name you and your children and your children's children will have reason to pronounce with blessing. And as but few of you probably knew him or ever saw him, for it is almost forty years since he removed from Roxbury, and more than twenty since his death, you will expect me to satisfy that affectionate curiosity with which we seek to know the smallest circumstance in the personal history of one who, though unknown to us, has yet by some word or act powerfully interested us, or awakened in an unusual degree emotions of admiration or love or gratitude. I am sorry that I must disappoint you, that I have only a most meagre account to offer; a few isolated facts, with here and there a date, is all that I can give you. But this will not seem strange, when you consider how many are to-day living good and useful lives, of whom twenty years after their death you would be able to learn little more than the place and date of their birth and burial.

> "The evil that men do lives after them;
> The good is oft interred with their bones."

Caleb Fellowes, the founder of this Athenæum, was born in Gloucester, Massachusetts, on the 9th of July, 1771, one hundred and two years ago to a day. His father was Cornelius Fellowes, and the maiden name of his mother, a Roxbury lady, was Sarah Williams. Of his youth we know nothing except that he early showed a passion for the sea — passion that proved irresistible as he grew older; and at last, in spite of the wishes of his parents, young Caleb shipped on board a vessel bound for China. It is said that he run away from the ship in which he sailed, when she had touched at some island in the Indian Ocean, and that he was afterwards impressed into the East India service, and acted as pilot for some time on the coast of Hindostan. It is certain that for twenty-five years nothing was heard of him, and he was supposed to be lost. But in the mean time he had settled at Calcutta, where he made many friends, and where, by honorable trade, he accumulated considerable property. In 1812 he returned to this country, and lived for a number of years in Philadelphia, where, at the age of fifty-three, he married Mrs. Sarah Carver.* Four years later he came to live in Roxbury, and occupied the house at the corner of Shawmut avenue and Bartlett street, which after 1836 was the home of Dr. Henry Bartlett.

I pause at the mention of that name, not to praise him whom my praise could not exalt in your affection or esteem, nor yet to pay to his memory that tribute of personal gratitude which the recollection of his tender sympathy and his precious help in more than one dark hour

*Her maiden name I have not been able to learn. She was born in Philadelphia, and there she died on the second of August, 1865, at the age of eighty-seven, having survived her husband thirteen years. Her bequest to the Fellowes Athenæum, together with the accumulated interest, amounts to $33,000, and the whole of this sum is now available for the purchase of books.

would prompt; — no, only to utter the wish, so natural, and yet how vain, that his life might have been spared to witness, in the completion of this building and its formal dedication, the realization of cherished hopes. Doubtless it is known to many of you that, public-spirited as Dr. Bartlett always was, as a trustee of the Fellowes Fund he took an unusual, I may say an ardent, interest in the establishment of this library. It was to have stood, as you know, but a few steps from his own home, and I cannot doubt that, as the infirmities of age began to warn him that he must rest, he pleased himself often with the anticipation of many a quiet hour of enjoyment within these walls, renewing that acquaintance with favorite authors which the arduous toils of a profession, to which he gave himself without stint, so greatly interrupted. But alas! that was not to be. We feel his absence from among us to-day with renewed sorrow; but we also rejoice in the recollection of his virtues. The upright citizen, the true friend, the good physician, the noble man.*

But to return to my narrative, which I had almost ended. The old longing for the sea returned, and in 1834 Mr. Fellowes sailed a second time for India, but now only for a brief absence. The following year he returned to Philadelphia, and there lived with his wife in great domestic happiness till his eighty-second year. He died on the eighth of November, 1852, leaving the greater part of his property for the founding of this library, which will henceforth bear his name and give testimony to his wise liberality.

Such is the meagre record of a life not unmarked by adventure, but otherwise not differing outwardly from that of thousands — simple, unostentatious, useful. Of the character of Mr. Fellowes you will already have inferred much, and you will be able to judge more from this portrait, which I am assured is a singularly faithful likeness. He is described as a man of dignified but gentle manners, and amiable and affectionate disposition. I should say that this likeness clearly indicates superior intelligence, with natural refinement and benignity of nature, and that the form of the chin and the lines about the mouth give unmistakable evidence of firmness and decision. Indeed, an incident of his second voyage to India proves that in this last particular we are not deceived. The ship in which Mr. Fellowes sailed was within a few leagues of port, and a pilot had already been taken on board, when one of those fearful typhoons that sometimes sweep the Indian seas suddenly burst upon the waves and the ship. The practised eye of Mr. Fellowes saw the imminent danger, saw the bewilderment of the pilot, and warned him that the vessel was driving upon the Western Reef. This warning was unheeded, and as the peril grew each moment more deadly, he

* Dr. Henry Bartlett was born Nov. 9th, 1801, and died at Roxbury, July 20th, 1872.

thrust the pilot from the helm, grasped it with his own hands, and shouted his orders in their own tongue to the Lascars, who tremblingly obeyed, and in a few hours the ship was brought safe to her anchorage.

"But why," I imagine you will ask, "should Mr. Fellowes bequeath his fortune to us, to whom he was bound by no strong tie, and who had no claim upon his bounty?" As you have seen he was not born in Roxbury, no part of his youth was passed here; and here accordingly none of those early associations could have been formed, which are commonly the most delightful, and on which in his old age he would most love to dwell. His early manhood was spent among a strange people, on the shores of another continent; and the last period of his life in a distant city, surrounded by those who respected and loved him. There too he had found the greatest of all his blessings, the dear companion of many peaceful years, the comfort and stay of his old age; her who, when he was gone, sealed her sacred wifely devotion to his memory by bestowing her own wealth on the institution which was to be founded by the beneficence of her husband. Strange then it may well seem, that you should be the chosen object of his favor; and it might easily have been otherwise. Mr. Fellowes not unnaturally thought of the city where he had found a happy home for almost twenty years; and being in his later life a great reader, he designed to found there an institution which should be to many the means of that enjoyment and culture which he had himself derived from the best literature. But fortunately, before he was fully resolved, he asked the advice of a friend with whom he had lived in Roxbury in the most intimate relations. That friend survives him in a vigorous old age, and he is present with us to-day. You all know him well, — the faithful steward of his friend's legacy to you, your friend and neighbor, and mine, the friend of everybody, — Supply Clapp Thwing. He said to Mr. Fellowes — I give his own words — "My friend, your mother was born in Roxbury, and there, you say yourself, you passed some of the happiest years of your life. We want an Athenæum, and you could not leave your property, outside of your own family, to a better object." Few words, but fit and effective. For the following year, on reading the will of his friend, Mr. Thwing had the satisfaction of finding that his appeal was successful. We are forbidden by religion and by philosophy to indulge in feelings of envy; but I will confess that I do, with all my heart, envy a good man the satisfaction that he must feel in knowing that through his act a great and lasting good has been conferred upon his fellow-citizens.

But I have omitted one circumstance, without which my account would be incomplete; and yet I know not if I have a right to disclose what was told me, perhaps in confidence, months ago, and what I dared not ask permission to make known, when I saw that the public interests demanded that the whole truth should be told. I say "the public interest," for it does concern the public to know of every noble and unselfish act which makes nobleness and unselfishness easier for all. And it is due to Mr. Thwing, though I may offend him by this disclosure, that you should know that the planting of this institution among you is due not less to his disinterestedness than to his timely and prudent counsel. You will already have surmised something of what I had to tell you, namely, that a large part of the sum which, together with the accumulated interest, has been devoted to the establishment of this library, was by Mr. Fellowes's first will bequeathed to Mr. Thwing; and that it was at his urgent request, when this became known to him, that his friend cancelled the legacy and increased by so much his bequest to you. Thus happily what the splendid generosity of the one conceived and begun, the rare unselfishness of the other completed and crowned; and hence, while we shall always hold him in grateful remembrance to whom we owe this noble benefaction, we shall honor in our hearts the not less noble self-sacrifice of him who refused wealth proffered in the name of friendship, that he might bestow enduring riches on us, and on those who shall come after us; or, still better, that he might put it in the power of each and all of us to enrich ourselves. We have a mine which we can work if we will. Here is gold which we can have for the quarrying; and, unlike those who dig in Californian or Australian mines, we may be sure that patient, earnest, persistent toil will meet a rich reward.

It was my design to speak of the relation of the library to the school; to show how the one supplements and completes the work of the other; to show how to the knowledge and discipline which it is the function of the school to impart, the library may add that culture which it is the peculiar office of literature to contribute. For, while science may train the reason and art foster the love of the beautiful, literature must everlastingly remain the most potent instrument of general culture. But I have already greatly exceeded the time within which I was commanded to limit my remarks, and I will not longer trespass upon the time of the gentleman who is to follow, and whom you are impatient to hear.

The Honorable George S. Hillard, one of the Trustees of the Public Library, being introduced, spoke as follows: —

I find it set down in the bills that I shall speak on behalf of the Trustees of the Public Library. My friend, Mr. Greenough, the President of the Board of Trustees, has already spoken on behalf of that body, and has said, it seems to me, all that the occasion demands, and anything from me appears like a work of supererogation.

In discharging the duty here assigned to me, I am embarrassed not by the poverty but by the wealth of my theme. There are many subjects which present themselves to our consideration, but a due regard to the brevity of human life requires me to do no more than touch lightly upon a very few.

I am one of the Trustees of the Public Library. We are chosen by the City Council, and the City Council is elected annually by the citizens of Boston. We are thus the servants of the public, and at one remove, its immediate servants. We must obey the will of our masters, and if we do not, they will find others who will. We are thus under the control of that power called public sentiment, which, like the air we breathe, is hardly felt when at rest, but when roused sweeps everything before it with irresistible sway. We have charge of the central institution in Boston proper, and its affiliated Branches in East Boston, South Boston, and in what you will permit me to call Roxbury, for I am too old to learn or unlearn any new tricks of speech. Our duties involve some labor and some responsibility. Among other things, we are required to select the books which are to be read by this community; of course, in making such selection we must consult the taste of the public which has set us this work to do; in other words, we must buy such books as the public wants to read. But we do not feel that our duty stops here. We wish, while we are consulting and obeying the public taste, to do what we can to elevate that taste, and make it crave for its intellectual food a higher class of books.

We think that in thus doing we are obeying that spirit of enlightened philanthropy to which the Public Library owes its birth. For in founding this institution it was not intended to furnish intellectual entertainment merely. It was intended to supplement and extend that intellectual culture which is begun and carried out to a certain degree in the public schools. And these public schools themselves owe their birth to a similar spirit of far-seeing philanthropy and enlightened statesmanship. When for the first time the government of the country was entrusted to the people of the country it was felt by wise and good men that in order to discharge this trust worthily, the people should be at once intelligent and virtuous. It has been an honorable fact in the history of our country that from the beginning its favored classes have recognized the duty of promoting the more intellectual training of the community generally.

I am old enough to embrace within my memory a whole half-century;

I have thus reached an age when men are permitted to be garrulous and pardoned if they are dull. When I recall the changes that have taken place, and the progress which has been made, I feel as if I must be the "Wandering Jew," and that I have lived centuries instead of years. When I first remember Boston, it was a small town of about 40,000 inhabitants, and Roxbury was truly a rural district where we boys used to go bird's-nesting and huckleberrying. I hope the boys of to-day do the latter and not the former. The schools and means of education at that time, compared with what they are to-day, were like the steamboat as compared with the canoe, and I can hardly find language strong enough to set forth the scarcity of books at that time, compared with their abundance to-day. Books were then a rare luxury, and they were valued and enjoyed accordingly.

But there is no unmixed good in this world. For every blessing we are also called into judgment. If by reason of far better schools, and a far greater abundance of books, domestic education is neglected, then these schools and these books are by no means an unqualified good. For the best education is the education of the mother's lap and the mother's knee, the education of the domestic hearth. There is no better preparation than the nurture and training of a virtuous and happy household. The habits of mutual accommodation, the habitual small self-sacrifices, the honorable preference of one to another, which are found in the happy home, are of the greatest value in the formation of character. These blessings are hardly ever properly appreciated, except by those who have missed them. The great and good Dr. Arnold said that in his school his object was, to make his pupils, first, Christians, second, gentlemen, and third, scholars. This is giving to character, so called, a higher place than to intellect, as it should have, and this should be the aim of all persons who are, directly or indirectly, occupied with the duty of educating the people.

We have here, my friends, a building singularly well adapted to the purposes for which it was intended. I presume it is the best library building in New England, with the best arrangements for the accommodation and distribution of books. It has got, sooner or later, to be filled with books. In determining what books should be here for circulation, we want your aid and co-operation, and especially the aid of such of you as are parents. Books may be divided into three classes,— some are good, some are bad, and many are neither good nor bad. Bad books are the source of infinite evil; but, of course, we don't propose to have any books here which are positively bad. But, remember, that the reading of indifferent books is merely intellectual pastime, and does nothing to enrich the mind or train the character; and among these books which are neither good nor bad, are many the character of which you will understand when I call them sensational. These books are to proper intellectual food what brandy and confectionery are to beef and bread. They stimulate, but they do not invigorate. The great objection to them is, that they give unreal pictures of life and its duties. I rarely go to the theatre without saying to myself, How unlike this all is to real life. Things do not happen in the world as they do upon the stage, and I have the same feeling generally in reading works of fiction. From my own observation I should say, that the reading of our young people lies too much among works of this class, commended as many of them are by high literary power. They give false views of life, invest it with a rose-colored atmosphere; but this daily life of ours is a grave and serious thing, full of cares and toils, demanding patience, endurance, and submission, and is not the fairy world of fiction. The discontent, produced by the comparison between this ideal world and the real world upon whose rocks we are thrown, is a fruitful source of unhappiness.

And now, in conclusion, the moral of my discourse is, that we want the co-operation of the fathers and mothers of this community, in the duty of furnishing books for their children to read. We want them to exercise a supervision over the books which their children read; we want them to encourage their children in the reading of books which are positively good, and to discourage them in the reading of those which are worthless. Let them, by precept and example, induce them to read such books as shall help them to become good men and good women, good husbands and good wives, good fathers and good mothers; and thus the hope and purpose of those to whose bounty we owe the Public Library shall be accomplished.

The MAYOR, in conclusion, announced that the delivery of books would begin in the course of the following week; and at a quarter of five o'clock he pronounced the ceremonies closed.

The company were now allowed an opportunity to inspect the building.

APPENDIX.

The Will of Caleb Fellowes, dated at Philadelphia, July 15, 1852, has the following clauses: —

I desire my executors to pay and deliver the funds or balance in their hands to the twelve trustees who may be appointed under the directions and requests hereinafter given and named by me, and for the uses and purposes hereinafter specified.

In order, to the extent of my ability, that I may benefit and please the inhabitants of Roxbury, in Massachusetts, as well as any worthy persons who may visit that city, I propose by this will to provide for an Athenæum to be established there; and for the establishment and maintenance of it, I desire that twelve inhabitants of Roxbury and their successors, may be incorporated as Trustees of the said Athenæum, by the Legislature or judicial authorities of Massachusetts. Accordingly, on the decease of my wife, I desire my executors to transmit an official copy of this my last will to Supply Clapp Thwing, William Whiting and Rev. George Putnam, of Roxbury, Massachusetts; and I request them and the survivors and survivor of them, thereupon to apply by petition or otherwise to the Legislature or judicial authorities of Massachusetts, requesting them to charter or incorporate twelve of the inhabitants of Roxbury (of whom I request that the said Supply Clapp Thwing, William Whiting and Rev. George Putnam may be three), and their successors forever, as Trustees for the following purposes, namely: —

1. To receive from my executors the residuary funds that may remain in their hands after the settlement and confirmation of their accounts as hereinbefore provided for,

2. In case the said residuary funds shall not amount to forty-five thousand dollars, to keep these funds safely invested until the principal and interest shall amount to forty-five thousand dollars.

3. Whenever forty-five thousand dollars shall be available, to lay out and expend forty thousand dollars thereof in purchasing a suitable lot of ground, within half a mile of the Rev. Mr. Putnam's meeting-house in Roxbury, and in erecting upon it a building or edifice for an Athe-

næum; the plan of which I desire to be as nearly as practicable like that of the Philadelphla Athenæum, and to be used, as that institution is, for literary and instructive purposes.

To keep the sum or surplus above the said forty thousand dollars constantly and safely invested and to expend the income of the said surplus half yearly forever in purchasing and supplying books and periodicals for the Athenæum. I confide in the the said Supply Clapp Thwing, William Whiting and Rev. George Putnam, and the survivors and survivor of them, that in the act of incorporation or in the by-laws of the Trustees, all proper provisions shall be made for keeping the building in repair, and for the appointment and remuneration of such persons as it may be needful to employ for the establishment. There are two provisions, however, respecting which I will express my own wishes and opinions. I desire that by any charter or act of incorporation it may be provided that vacancies by death or otherwise in the Board of Trustees shall be filled by the surviving or continuing Trustees, or by a majority of them. The other provision relates to the number of the Trustees, and twelve has been mentioned; but I wish it to be understood that I leave the decision as to the number to others; barely saying that I think it should not be less than five or more than twelve.

5. All the rest and residue of my personal estate and funds remaining in the hands of my executors after the decease of my wife, and after the settlement and confirmation of the accounts of my executors, I give and bequeath to Supply Clapp Thwing, William Whiting and Rev. George Putnam, and the survivors or survivor of them, and to such other persons as may be with them incorporated as hereinbefore provided for, and to their successors forever in trust for the uses, intents and purposes hereinbefore specified; and I direct my executors to deliver the said residuary estate and funds to the said Supply Clapp Thwing, William Whiting, Rev. George Putnam and their associates, as soon as they shall have been incorporated as Trustees for the purposes aforesaid, etc.

The Will of SARAH FELLOWES, dated the 11th April, 1861, contains the following clauses: —

I hereby direct my executor to hold the residue of my estate and invest the same as he may deem best, until a charter shall have been obtained for an Athenæum in Roxbury, Massachusetts, as provided for in the last will and testament of my late husband, Caleb Fellowes, deceased, which will was duly proven and recorded, etc. Reference is hereby made to said will for the full particulars in regard to said Athenæum. I hereby will and direct that so soon as the building provided to be erected according to the said will of my said husband has been completed, after obtaining said charter or act of incorporation, then my executor herein named shall pay over to Supply Clapp Thwing, William Whiting and Rev. George Putnam, and the survivor or survivors of them, the whole of the residue of my estate as aforesaid, to be received and held by them, and the survivors or survivor of them, and their successors in trust, for the following uses and purposes, that is to say, to be applied to the purchase of such books and periodicals as the managers of said Athenæum at Roxbury, Massachusetts, may from time to time deem best to be placed in said Athenæum as the property thereof, etc.

The FELLOWES ATHENÆUM became legally organized finally under the following authority: —

ACT OF INCORPORATION.

COMMONWEALTH OF MASSACHUSETTS.

In the year one thousand eight hundred and sixty-six.

AN ACT to incorporate the Trustees of the Fellowes Athenæum in Roxbury.

Be it enacted by the Senate and House of Representatives in General Court assembled, and by the authority of the same, as follows: —

SECTION 1. Supply C. Thwing, William Whiting, and George Putnam, and their associates and successors, are hereby made a Corporation by the name of the "Trustees of the Fellowes Athenæum in Roxbury," and they and their successors, and such as shall be duly elected members of said Corporation, shall be and remain a Corporation by that name forever, with all the powers and privileges, and subject to all the duties, restrictions, and liabilities, imposed by all general laws that are or may be hereafter in force concerning such corporations. And the said Trustees may elect such officers as may be found necessary, fix the tenure of their office, frame such by-laws as may be deemed expedient, and elect new members of said Corporation, provided that the whole number of Trustees shall not exceed twelve.

SECT. 2. The said Corporation shall have power to receive legacies bequeathed to said Trustees by the late Caleb Fellowes and Sarah Fellowes of Philadelphia; and to perform and carry out the trusts upon which they were given by the respective wills of Caleb Fellowes and Sarah Fellowes, and they may hold other real and personal property not exceeding two hundred thousand dollars in value, of which the income shall be appropriated exclusively to literary, scientific and educational purposes.

SECT. 3. This act shall take effect upon its passage.

HOUSE OF REPRESENTATIVES, Feb'y 12, 1866.
(*Signed*) JAMES M. STONE,
Speaker.

IN SENATE, Feb'y 14, 1866.
Passed to be enacted.
(*Signed*) JOSEPH A. POND,
President.

Feb'y 15, 1866.
Approved.
(*Signed*) ALEX. H. BULLOCK.

SECRETARY'S DEPARTMENT, Boston, Feb'y 21, 1866.
A true copy.
(*Signed*) OLIVER WARNER,
(SEAL.) *Secretary of the Commonwealth.*

At a meeting of the Trustees of the Fellowes Fund, March 12, 1866, the ACT OF INCORPORATION was accepted; and S. C. THWING was appointed Secretary to act as Chairman with power to call meetings, etc., and HENRY BARTLETT, JOSEPH S. ROPES, and JOHN FELT OSGOOD were chosen members of the Board.

At a meeting of the Trustees, 18th April, 1866, S. C. THWING was chosen Treasurer; JOHN F. OSGOOD, Secretary; and JOSEPH S. ROPES and JOHN F. OSGOOD were associated with the Treasurer as a Committee of Finance.

At a meeting of the Trustees, 16th December, 1871, the Rev. GEORGE PUTNAM was duly elected PRESIDENT of the BOARD OF TRUSTEES. The Treasurer reported that the funds amounted to $54,000, and it was

Voted, That the President be authorized to communicate with the City Government relative to combining the interests of the Fellowes Athenæum with those of the proposed Branch of the Public Library to be located in this district.

Henry Bartlett and John F. Osgood were chosen a committee to purchase a suitable lot of land to build upon.

Under the authority of the vote already given, the President of the Fellowes Trustees addressed the Mayor and City Council, asking for a hearing before the appropriate committee, and in the presence of the Trustees of the Public Library. This communication was referred to the Committee of the City Council on the Public Library, and that committee, through Alderman George D. Ricker, Chairman *pro tempore*, reported in the Board of Aldermen, December 26th, 1871, a form of indenture, which passed the City Council, December 30th, and the Honorable William Gaston, the Mayor of the City, gave it his signature, January 26th, 1872; and under the authority given by the Board of Trustees of the Fellowes Athenæum, January 22d, 1872, it was also signed by George Putnam, their President.

The agreement reads as follows: —

This indenture between the City of Boston and the Trustees of the Fellowes Athenæum in Roxbury, a corporation duly created by law, witnesseth: —

That, whereas the said Trustees hold certain funds under the will of Caleb Fellowes, late of Philadelphia, in the State of Pennsylvinia, deceased, in trust, to lay out and expend forty thousand dollars upon land, and a building to be erected thereon, within half a mile of the meeting-house of the First religious society in Roxbury, to be used for an Athenæum for literary and instructive purposes for the benefit and pleasure of the inhabitants of said Roxbury and of other worthy persons who may visit that city:

And in further trust, to keep the remainder of said sum over and above said forty thousand dollars, constantly and safely invested, and to expend the income thereof, half yearly forever, in purchasing and supplying books and periodical works for the said Athenæum:

And whereas it is expedient that the City of Boston should establish in that part of said city called Roxbury, and formerly the City of Roxbury, a Branch of its Public Library:

And whereas, the said City and the said Trustees can accomplish the purposes of said Athenæum and of said Public Library more effectually in conjunction than separately, and have accordingly agreed upon a method of co-operation so as to bring about a union of the resources of the two institutions:

And whereas, in order to furnish the needful accommodations for the united institutions, it may be necessary for the said Trustees to expend somewhat more than forty thousand dollars upon land and building, and in that case they will be obliged to treat the surplus as an investment of which the income is to be applied for the purchase of books as aforesaid:

And whereas, upon the completion of said building, the said Trustees will become entitled to a further sum under the will of Sarah Fellowes, upon trust, to be applied to the purchase of such books and periodicals as the said Trustees may from time to time deem best to be placed in said Athenæum, as the property thereof:

Now, therefore, it is agreed between the parties hereto as follows, viz.: —

The said Trustees shall proceed as soon as may be to erect a building which shall contain suitable accommodations for a Branch Public Library of the City of Boston as well as for said Athenæum.

As soon as said building shall be ready for occupancy, the said City shall appropriate towards a Branch Public Library, for the territory now comprising Wards 13, 14 and 15, as large a sum of money as has been, or shall be, appropriated for outfit and maintenance to any other Branch Library in said city, and the said City shall pay for the rental of said building the sum of sixteen hundred dollars per annum, which shall be paid annually to the said Trustees, to be laid out by them, after paying insurance, repairs, etc., in the purchase of books and periodicals, to be the property of said Trustees of the Fellowes Athenæum in Roxbury, and their successors in said trust.

The rest of said appropriation shall be expended in the purchase of books and the administration and management of the joint institutions by the Trustees of the Public Library.

All books and periodicals purchased by the said Trustees of the Athenæum from any of the funds in their hands for the purchase of books as aforesaid, shall be put in charge of the custodians of the said Branch Public Library, being first distinctly marked as the property of said Trustees, and shall be subject to the direction of the Trustees of the Public Library, as to custody, care, and arrangement within the said building, and shall be open to the public for reading and circulation under such regulations as the said Trustees of the Public Library may, with the consent of the said Trustees of the Fellowes Athenæum, from time to time establish.

This contract shall be terminable by either party, at any time, upon giving six months' notice to the other party, and, upon its termination, the books shall belong to the party which shall have purchased them, or to whom they have been given; the furniture, shelving, and all other movable property, which shall have been purchased by the City, shall belong to the said City; and the property which shall have been fixed to the real estate, and any furniture which may have been purchased by the said Trustees of the Fellowes Athenæum, shall belong to the said Trustees.

A suitable room shall be provided by the Trustees of the Fellowes Athenæum, in the building to be erected by them, and furnished by the City, for the joint use of the Trustees of the Fellowes Athenæum and the Trustees of the Public Library.

It is further agreed that all questions of detail of management, not herein provided for, shall be settled in conjunction by the Trustees of the Fellowes Athenæum and of the Public Library.

This was again modified by the following agreement, which was executed in consequence of an order of the City Council, authorizing the Mayor to sign such a supplemental indenture as may be approved by the Trustees of the Public Library: —

This INDENTURE, made this twelfth day of April, in the year of our Lord one thousand eight hundred and seventy-two, between the City of Boston and the Trustees of the Fellowes Athenæum, in Roxbury, a corporation duly created by law,

Witnesseth: —

That the contract entered into by the said parties by an Indenture, duly executed, dated the twenty-ninth day of January, in the year one thousand eight hundred and seventy-two, shall be and hereby is changed and altered by striking out and expunging from the said Indenture the words "with the consent of the said Trustees of the Fellowes Athenæum," in the paragraph relating to the custody, care, arrangement, reading and circulation of books and periodicals purchased by said Trustees; and also by striking out and expunging the paragraph in said Indenture which is in the following words, viz.: "A suitable room shall be provided by the Trustees of the Fellowes Athenæum, in the building to be erected by them and furnished by the City for the joint use of the Trustees of Fellowes Athenæum, and the Trustees of the Public Library" — and the said Indenture shall be construed for all purposes as though the words and provisions, hereby agreed to be stricken out and expunged, had not been inserted therein.

In witness whereof the said parties have caused their seals to be hereto affixed and these presents to be signed by William Gaston, Mayor of said City, and George Putnam, President of said Trustees, respectively, the day and year first above written.

City of Boston,

By WILLIAM GASTON, *Mayor.* [Seal.]

In presence of
James R. Carret.

The Trustees of the Fellowes Athenæum,

By GEORGE PUTNAM, *Pres't.*

Approved, by vote of the Trustees of the Public Library.

By W. W. GREENOUGH,
Pres't of the Board.

At a meeting of the Fellowes Trustees, 19th Feb., 1872, Nathaniel J. Bradlee was added to the Board, and later, 12th March, Henry Bartlett, John F. Osgood, and Nathaniel J. Bradlee were chosen to act as a Building Committee. Dr. Bartlett died July 20th, 1872, when the chairmanship devolved upon Mr. Osgood.

A lot upon Bartlett street, not far from Shawmut avenue, had been bought; the plans for a building had been drawn under the direction of Mr. Bradlee, as the architect, and the erection begun under contract, when it became desirable on account of the purchase by the Metropolitan Horse Railroad Company of the surrounding land, for the erection of stables, to sell this site, under a special agreement, to that company. Accordingly, in August, the work on the new building was stopped.

Some delay was experienced in finding another suitable location, but the lot bounded by Millmont street, Lambert avenue and Lambert street, measuring one hundred and

FRONT ELEVATION, ON MILLMONT STREET.

56'4"
LIBRARY 27X55 4"
53'4"
81 6"
LIBRARIAN'S R.
15 X 18
COUNTER
COUNTER
CT.
WAITING
ROOM
FOR
FOR
36
37
ADULTS AND
GIRLS
BOYS
TRUSTEES R.
15 X 20'8
VESTIBULE 8X36'8"
23'2"
UP
18'4"
18'4"

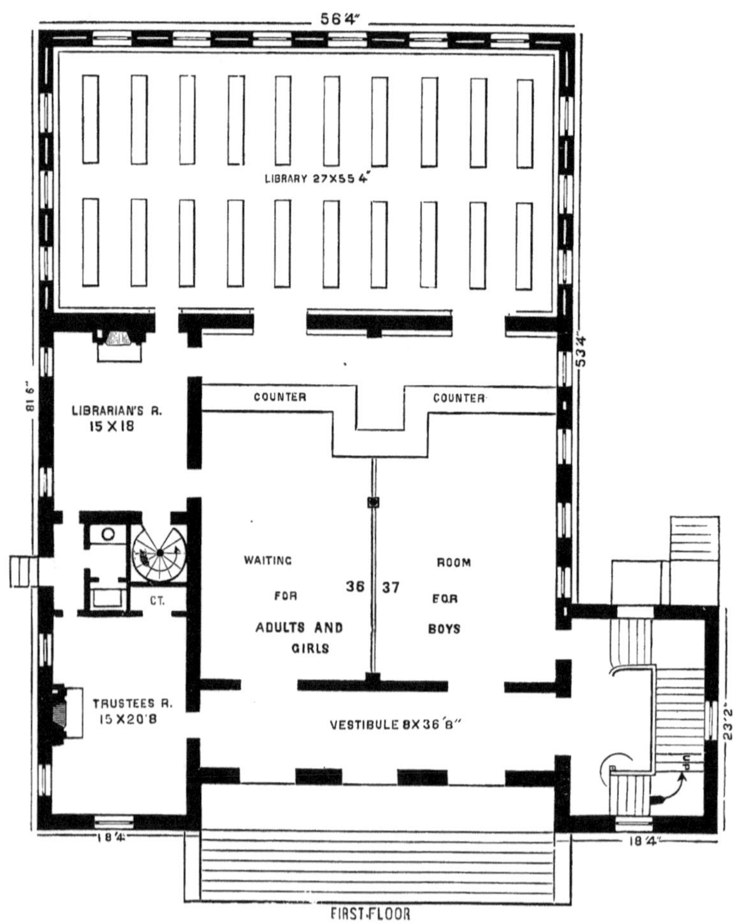

FIRST-FLOOR

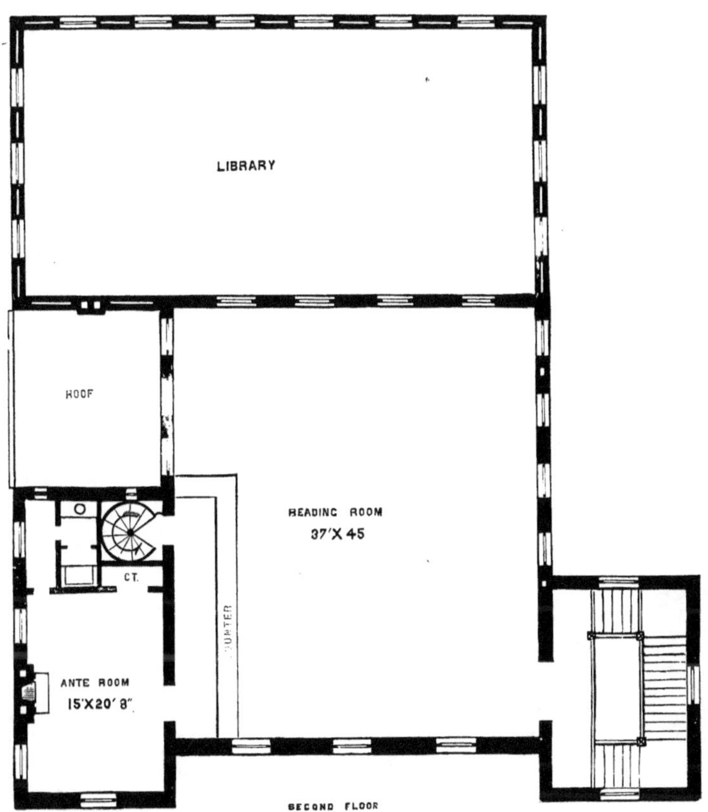

SECOND FLOOR

twenty-four by one hundred and twenty-six feet, and containing 15,933 square feet, having been secured, ground was broken on the new site late in September, 1872, and the erection of the building was begun, substantially upon the arrangement before adopted (which will be seen in the engraved plans, given in the Report of the Trustees of the Public Library for 1872); but with some minor changes, which are embodied in the plans engraved for the present publication. The change of site involved one alteration not shown by comparison of the plans. The library room proper, which in the original design had the same altitude as the front portion of the building, was lowered so as still to give a clear space of twenty-four feet to the ceiling, enough to allow of two additional floors, whenever it becomes desirable to augment its storage capacity, which at the utmost is reckoned at one hundred thousand volumes. This diminution of the altitude of the rear of the building was called for by the rapid falling off of the ground toward Lambert street, which would have given the original plan an unsightly elevation above the street. The same cause also secured a light and airy basement, not possible on the level site, which has been turned to good account in part for the Janitor's lodgings, and which is capable of much increasing the capacity and working space of the Library, if ever needed. The more open position of the new structure rendered other changes in the externals of the building desirable, which have increased its cost by about four thousand dollars over the original estimates.

The building has a granite foundation, with steps of the same at the main entrance, and is built of brick, with freestone trimmings. The various contractors for the work were as follows: —

Ivory Bean,	for the	Mason Work.
Lanning and Drisco,	" "	Carpenter's Work.

G. W. and F. Smith,	for the	Iron Work.
Edward F. Meany,	" "	Free-stone Work.
C. H. Hardwick,	" "	Granite Work.
L. D. Winn,	" "	Plastering Work.
Hicks and Badger,	" "	Copper Work.
C. S. Parker and Sons,	" "	Slating and Tinning.
John Everbeck,	" "	Painting and Glazing.
Wallburg and Sherry,	" "	Fresco Work.
C. S. Clogston & Co.,	" "	Steam Heating.
S. A. Stetson & Co.,	" "	Gas Pipes.
Lockwood and Lumb,	" "	Plumbers.

The land on Bartlett street, which had cost $9,000, and consisted of 10,000 square feet, was transferred to the Metropolitan Railroad Company, upon their agreement to pay for an equivalent area elsewhere, at $1.50 per foot. The present site being of larger area (15,933 square feet), necessitated an additional outlay of $933, which with the cost of the land as first bought, has made the charges for the land amount to $9,933. The total expenditures of the Building Committee have been about $40,000, making a grand total of $49,933.

During the progress of affairs the following additional members were chosen by the Board of Trustees of the Fellowes Athenæum: SAMUEL C. COBB, in place of Dr. BARTLETT deceased; CHARLES K. DILLAWAY and WILLIAM C. COLLAR, on the 20th September, 1872; and the Reverend EDWARD E. HALE, on the 2d of January, 1873.

The PUBLIC LIBRARY of Boston, which had been founded in 1852, sought to extend its usefulness, when, in 1870, it established its first Branch at East Boston. A circulation of 75,000 volumes the first year confirmed the views of the Trustees, and they have been further strengthened by the circulation of over 100,000, which was maintained at South Boston, the first year after the establishment of that Branch in May, 1872.

The Trustees of the Public Library were already contemplating the opening of a Branch in Roxbury, when the overtures were made by the Trustees of the Fellowes Athenæum; and shortly after the agreement had been made, the collection of books was begun at the Central Library, to be in readiness for transfer when wanted. Between six and seven hundred volumes were, early in the summer of 1872, selected from the duplicates of the Lower Hall and of the Duplicate Room; and to these have been added, chiefly by purchase, about 3,300 volumes, to constitute the portion contributed by the Public Library to the collection, with which the institution should begin its work. In February, 1873, the Superintendent of the Public Library, under the direction of the Book Committee of the Fellowes Athenæum (the Rev. Dr. Putnam at first, then the Rev. Edward E. Hale, and again, the Rev. Dr. Putnam) began the purchase of the more costly books, which, by the plan of union, it became the part of the Athenæum to provide; and these have amounted in the aggregate to over one thousand volumes. Thus, with almost five thousand volumes, the library begins its work.

A contract was made with J. J. McNutt, in January, 1873, for the shelving and other necessary furniture, by the Superintendent in behalf of the Trustees of the Public Library; and, as soon as was practicable, the authorities of the Public Library were informally put in charge of the building, June 16th, when the final arrangements were made for occupancy. The books were removed to it from the Central Library, June 20th and 21st, and the Reading Room for Periodicals was opened to the public, and the registration of applicants for cards, conveying the right to use the Library, was begun June 23d. The formal dedication followed, as already described, on the 9th of July; and all the necessary arrangements having been completed, the full use of the Library began with the delivery of books on the 16th of July.

www.ingramcontent.com/pod-product-compliance
Lightning Source LLC
LaVergne TN
LVHW011125110826
845150LV00008B/2251

* 9 7 8 1 4 1 8 1 9 5 4 5 8 *